FACEBOOK

POSTS ENGAGEMENT SECRETS

PROVEN STRATEGIES TO GET MORE LIKES, COMMENTS AND SHARES ON YOUR FACEBOOK POSTS

FACEBOOK POSTS ENGAGEMENT SECRETS

20 Proven Strategies to Get More Likes, Comments and Shares on Your Facebook Posts

Startup Jahswill

This book is part of the Facebook Business Series brought to you by StartUP Crest, a leading business development company with focus on startups and small businesses.

You can access more of our resources at

startupcrest.com

Take Your Business Online Facebook Group

Contact:info@startupcrest.com

+2348033867541

Table of Content

Introduction

Proven Strategies to Get More Likes, Comments and Shares on Your Facebook Posts

It's great that you now have a Facebook business page for your small business (well, if you have not gotten one, this may just be the right time to do so). You may or may not be making sales from Facebook yet. But, you really want to make consistent sales on Facebook.

You have heard about the Facebook algorithm that only posts with high engagement rates tend to do well by reaching more peope. Unfortunately, your posts don't get that high engagement. And your sales reflect that. What do you do?

This guide to the rescue!

So, let's dive in…

The Best Kept Secrets

Secret One

Ask for It

This may sound too easy and too obvious, but there is much power in asking. Even one of the Holy books says to keep asking and you shall be given.

Therefore, the first thing you want to do is ask your followers to engage with your posts. Ask them to "LIKE" a post if they truly like it. Tell them to share their thoughts, opinion and views by "COMMENTING" in the comments section.

For "SHARES", encourage them to share your post so that their friends and others can see it. You may want to sometime take it to the next level by saying stuff like "share so that more people who need this can see it, don't be selfish". It works like magic eh!

Secret Two

Use Different Types of Media

People react differently to different posts types. And different media elicit different emotions in people. Video posts tend to get higher engagement than photos and text in that order.

Infographics are also great post types as you are able to give people much information in a condensed format easy to digest.

In addition, the Facebook algorithm tends to favor video and photo content more than just text.

Pro Tip: When sharing video content on Facebook, don't make it too long. Five (5) minutes is usually great for people to watch to the end and engage easily.

So, mix things up by having different media types in your posts.

Secret Three

Use "Fill-in-the-Blank" Posts

These kinds of posts are usually in question format. If you can aim the right kind of question at the right audience, they will engage like fire in harmattan! It doesn't matter whether they are just text or images; "fill-in-the-blank" question posts are almost irresistible for most warm audience.

When done correctly, these will generate multiple times more comments than likes. And need I tell you that the Facebook algorithm gives more weight to comments than likes? Yeah, your posts can quickly blow through the roof with posts like these.

Now that's real engagement there!

Secret Four

Use Contests

Contests are great for engagements because everyone wants to win something. It may not be the price that is the motivation, but the bragging rights that "I won this"!

You don't have to hold contests every other day though. So that your followers will not become bored of take it for granted. A good strategy is to hold a regular contest on a regular day of the week or month.

If you are doing this on schedule, your followers will start looking forward to the day and contest. They may not wait for the post to show up in the newsfeeds but visit your page directly to participate.

I know it can be expensive to run contests and give away stuffs. But, they don't have to be any big prizes. They may even just be fun and trivial prizes such as "Fan of the week", or "Most like user post of the month".

The more trivial, fun and silly the prize, the more often you can run the contest. Then, once in awhile you can throw in a high-end prize to wow your followers.

Secret Five: Ask Questions

Yes, just that. When you ask a question, your audience knows that you expect an answer. Some will endeavor to respond to your question just to not look rude.

The secret is to ask simple questions. A "YES" or "NO" question is usually great for this purpose.

Pro Tip: And don't make the mistake of asking questions that will put your readers on the spot.

Secret Six

Help Followers Find Your Page Easily

If your followers don't visit your page directly, the chances of them engaging are highly reduced. Reason being that less and less of your posts is appearing on your followers' newsfeed.

One of the most common reasons given for never visiting a Page again is: "I couldn't figure out how to find it."

Let your followers know they can instantly access Pages (not just yours) by pointing out the options in navigation menu.

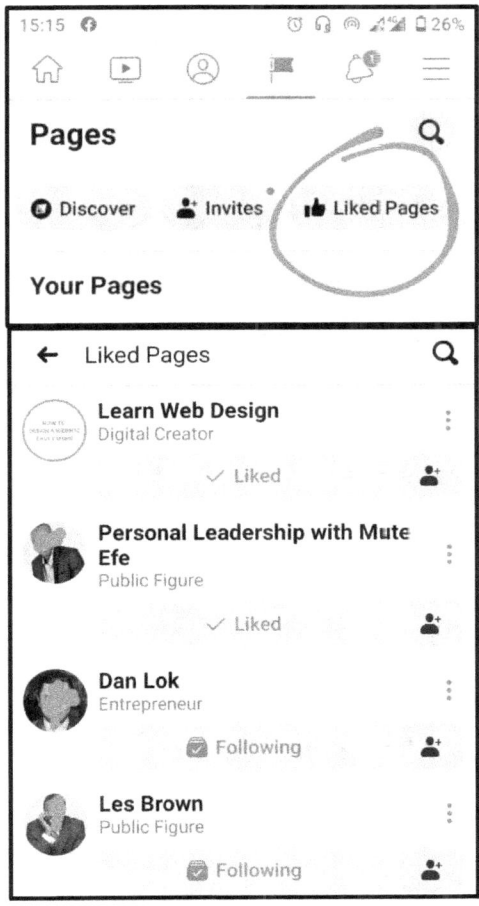

Secret Seven

Answer Questions Openly

For a small business, this could make or mar your efforts on Facebook! You are not very famous, so people will doubt you at first. That's why it's important you engage in comments section.

Respond to people's question in the comments section and only take conversations to dm if you must. This will also increase engagement rate for that particular post and increase sales.

The only exception to this may be a big celebrity that actually needs to discourage people getting too personal.

Secret Eight

Format Your Tabs for Engagement

If properly used, those little tabs can be prime real estate for your Facebook business page.

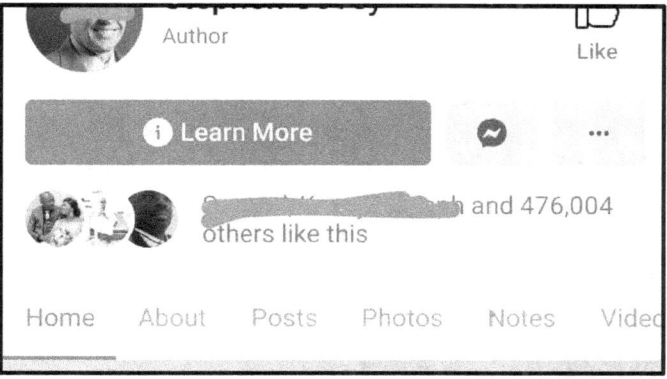

You should hide any irrelevant and unrelated tabs. Then arrange the tabs that will grab your followers attention at the top.

Secret Nine

Connect More, Sell Less

People use Facebook for social connection and entertainment. If your posts come across as always salesy and commercialized you will put your followers off – some may even be annoyed.

This will highly discourage engagement from your readers. Nobody wants to be sold to, but everybody desires friendship. So, instead of always posting about your products, post things that will breed connection.

Secret Ten

Use Quizzes

This is another powerful secret that the pros use to boost engagement.

They post quiz-like type of content that requires the reader to take some form of action.

Pro Tip: Add a personal touch to your quizzes to boost engagement further. Share your answer or other peoples answer to the quiz question to encourage your followers to also share their answers by commenting.

Secret Eleven

Recognize Top Followers

This plays on the human psychology. We all want to feel important and special in some respect. When you recognize one of your followers as a top fan for instance, they will feel good about it and may want to share that post on their own timeline.

They will comment and their friends too will congratulate them in the comments section.

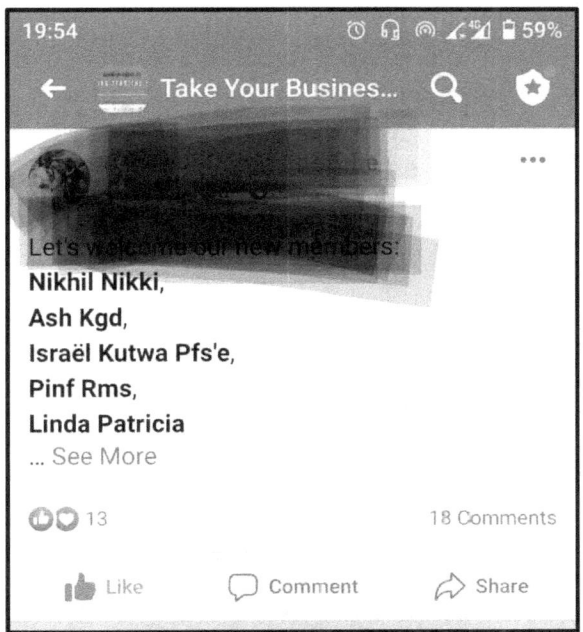

Now that's engagement there man!

Secret Twelve

Post Live (Be Around)

As much as possible, make posts as they are happening. If the events are current, the more engagement you will see.

You can schedule posts if you are going to be very busy and don't have someone managing your online activities who will be online always. However, make sure your scheduled posts are not out of context or outdated. This can happen if certain things occur that makes your scheduled post outdated.

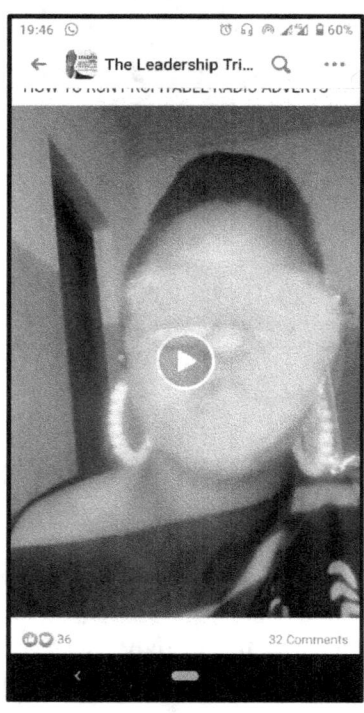

Pro Tip: Make sure you are monitoring your scheduled posts if you must schedule.

Secret Thirteen

Post a Cute Picture and Ask for Captions

A cute cat in the home-office? A new logo design or display picture? Or maybe you in a special holiday clothe. These kind of posts will move people to comment and like.

They work if you get the picture right for the right audience.

Secret Fourteen

Use Polls

Who doesn't like to share his or her opinion? We all believe we know more than we do, so every opportunity to air our opinion is almost always a welcome development.

Take advantage of this by polling your audience.

To get the best out of polls, just like asking questions, make sure they are simple and short. In addition, the options should not be too many, 2 or 3 is enough.

Secret Fifteen

Post High-Value Tips

A free tip is like free lunch. You will hardly find anyone who does not appreciate one.

The key is to share tips that are of high perceived value in the eyes of your reader. You don't want to post some general knowledge that everyone knows. Your aim is to get your audience so excited that they want to give you a thumbs-up or ask you for further help.

If you can master this art and are available to engage and connect, this secret alone can drive your engagement through the roof!

Secret Sixteen

Add Odd Photos to Your Posts

This is a special trick that the pros use regularly. They will share an unrelated picture along with a text post. Anyone who sees the picture will want to read the text. At the end of the post, they will tell you the post and photos are not necessarily related! Lol

The goal is to get your readers eyes popping and their minds racing thinking of what the post is all about.

People love the spectacular and the odd things seem to interest people more than the regular.

Secret Seventeen

Showcase Your Team

This could be a photo or video of your team member at work or having a swell time. It could also be a staff of the month contest and the winner showcased in your Facebook business page.

The staff member will want her friends to see this post. They will thus share it and comment on it. Their friends will join in the celebration by congratulating them in the comments section. Before you know what's happening, your engagement will be rising like a skyscraper.

Secret Eighteen

Be Human

People engage with people. The more human your followers see you, the more they will engage with your posts.

You can make mistake. A typo (can even be done on purpose) can generate so much engagement in a post that you will surprised why you have been spending so much time proofreading your posts!

Share a heartfelt experience, a sad story or a happy event in your own life.

Pro Tip: Make your writing style and tone be as natural as possible. Write as you would speak in everyday conversations.

Secret Nineteen

Surprise Your Audience Sometimes

How about a surprise free giveaway? An out of the blues special offer to one or more followers?

When you care for your followers like this, they will also care for you and will engage your posts always.

Secret Twenty

Drop the Odd Controversial Post

Controversy generates conversations and discussions. So, once in awhile drop that controversial post and let the arguments rage in the comments section.

Make sure you are posting something that your audience care about (avoid the emotionally charged topics though).

Pro Tip: If you want to play it safe, you can share another person's controversial post to your page.

Bonus Secret

Have a Behind-The-Scene Team

Have like 5 persons in your team who will always engage with your posts. The job of these guys is to like, comment and share all your posts.

This will 'trick' the Facebook algorithm to rank your post high and also encourage your 'real' followers to engage too.

About the Author

StartUP Jahswill

Entrepreneur | Public Speaker | Business Coach

Eduzobe Jahswill Udogbo (StartUP Jahswill) is a trained Physicist with a passion for building and growing small businesses.

He is the CEO of StartUP Crest, a company he formed to help young people start and grow small businesses. He is also the CEO of LabHub Medical Laboratories and Diagnostics and the founding Managing Partner/General Manager of Karone Photo World Ltd, both very successful startups.

In 2009 he setup his first registered company, SwiftTech Integrated Solutions Ltd with the aim of providing alternative power supply to residents of the satellite towns around the Nigerian capital territory, Abuja.

Although that venture turned out to be a total failure, Jahswill learned valuable lessons that have helped him to start and grow other businesses with varied degrees of success.

His number one desire is to help as many young people as possible to discover their entrepreneurial skills and use this to start and grow businesses that will provide employment and livelihood.

His mission is simple: help young people transition from frustrated job seekers and disillusioned startups to successful entrepreneurs.

He promotes financial education that helps young people understand the career options available to them as a means of creating wealth as opposed to the old one-way thinking of "Go to School, get a good job and live comfortably ever after"!

Jahswill appreciates that while university/college education might be a necessity in some chosen careers, it is just one of the options and not the surest path to creating wealth. That is why he advocates learning business and financial skills that gives the best and surest path to wealth creation. He spends most of his time developing content for his various educational platforms especially his blog www.startupcrest.com where he provides valuable resources for startups.

He is happily married and blessed with a beautiful daughter.

Other Books by the Author!

*No Bullshit Business Plan: How to Write a Business Plan Easily and Convincingly

*Facebook Marketing Mistakes: 14 Newbies Mistakes that are Holding Your business Down

*Facebook for Business Success: Top Secrets to Help You Run a Successful Business on Facebook

*Social Media Content to Cash: *Easily Create Content for Social Media (And Make Money from Your Content)*

*Take Your Business Online: *The Step-by-Step Guide to Taking Your Offline Business Online (Even if You Have No Tech Knowledge)*

Click Here to Get a Copy